THE HUMPBACK WHALE

BY
CARL R. GREEN
WILLIAM R. SANFORD

EDITED BY
DR. HOWARD SCHROEDER

**Professor in Reading and Language Arts
Dept. of Elementary Education
Mankato State University**

PRODUCED AND DESIGNED BY
BAKER STREET PRODUCTIONS
Mankato, MN

CRESTWOOD HOUSE
Mankato, Minnesota

LIBRARY OF CONGRESS CATALOGING IN PUBLICATION DATA

Green, Carl R.
  The humpback whale.

  SUMMARY: Examines the appearance, behavior, and life cycle of this playful singing whale and describes modern efforts to protect it.
  1. Humpback whale--Juvenile literature. (1. Humpback whale. 2. Whales) Sanford, William R. (William Reynolds). II. Schroeder, Howard. III. Baker Street Productions. IV. Title.
QL737.C424G74   1985   599.5'1   85-9645
ISBN 0-89686-274-7 (lib. bdg.)

International Standard Book Number:	Library of Congress Catalog Card Number:
Library Binding 0-89686-274-7	85-9645

ILLUSTRATION CREDITS:

Photos by William R. Curtsinger
Artwork by Bob Williams

CRESTWOOD HOUSE

Hwy. 66 South, Box 3427
Mankato, MN 56002-3427

Humpback's spout.

INTRODUCTION:

"Sure, I love to skin dive," Donny Black said. "But this is crazy. We're not really going to dive with a humpback whale, are we? That monster could swallow me in one gulp!"

Donny waited for his sister to tell him she was kidding. Instead, Sue calmly put on her swim fins. Well, this is her job, he thought. An oceanographer has to do daring things.

Sue had anchored their small boat well out to sea. Behind them, Donny could see the hills of Maui. This was his first visit to Hawaii. Yesterday, he had dived to watch the small reef fish.

Today was different. Sue pointed to a long, dark shape not far away. "There," she said, "that's Barney. I know him by the white spot on his tail. Remember, humpbacks never attack humans. Sure, they're giants. They grow to forty-five feet in length. And they weigh up to forty tons. But they're gentle giants."

Donny dived into the warm water. He cleared his face mask and swam after his sister. All at once Barney turned toward them. Donny could see the whale clearly now. The huge mammal was as big as a truck. Its long flippers sent it gliding toward them. Donny was ready to swim back to the boat.

4

An adult humpback whale is as big as a truck.

The humpback came closer. Donny saw one large, dark eye looking at him. The eye seemed wise and friendly. All at once, Donny's fear was gone. Barney was just as curious as he was!

Water swirled around him as Barney swam slowly by. The whale turned and came back for a second look. Donny took a deep breath and dived down to meet him.

Barney's black skin looked bumpy. As he came closer, Donny saw clumps of barnacles growing on

With a flip of its tail, the humpback is gone.

the whale's lip. Barnacles grow on boats, he thought. Why not on whales? The barnacles didn't seem to bother the humpback.

The second look was all Barney wanted. The humpback's great tail moved once and he headed out to deeper water. In a moment Barney was only a distant shadow. Donny turned back to the boat.

Sue was waiting for him. "What do you think of our friend?" she asked.

"I'll never forget him," Donny told her. He felt excited. "I want to know everything about humpbacks. How did they get their name? What do they eat? Where do they —"

Sue laughed. "Okay, slow down," she said. "I've been studying Barney and his friends. I'll tell you what I know . . ."

CHAPTER ONE:

Long ago, people thought whales were sea monsters. Their great size created many myths. Later on, people lost their fear of whales. They began to kill the huge mammals for their oil and meat.

The humpback whale was hunted almost to extinction. Over 100,000 humpbacks once lived in the oceans. Today, only about seven thousand are left. Just in time, most nations have agreed to protect these gentle giants of the sea. Humpbacks will survive — if everyone follows the rules.

Humpbacks belong to a large family

Humpbacks belong to a family known as the rorquals. Rorqual means "tubed whale." The "tubes" are deep grooves that run from the whale's throat to its belly. Humpbacks have an average of twenty-eight grooves, far less than other rorquals. When the whale feeds, these grooves open up like the folds that expand the sides of a briefcase. This expansion lets the whale scoop up huge mouthfuls of food in a single bite.

The humpback is a medium-sized rorqual. A blue whale is two times larger. Humpbacks also differ

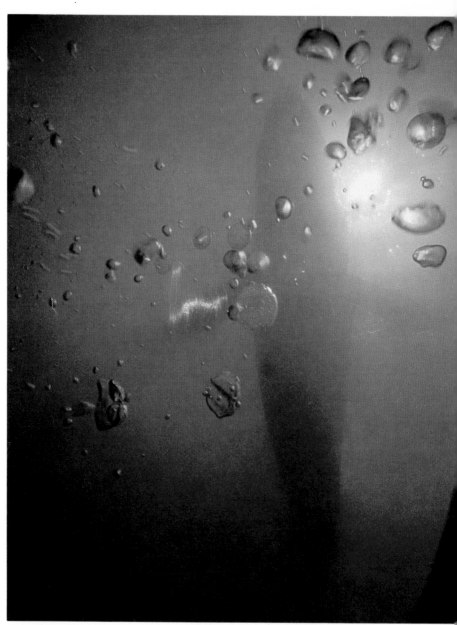

A humpback passes directly above a diver/photographer, showing its long flippers.

8

from other rorquals in another way. Most rorquals are graceful, fast swimmers. A humpback, however, has a larger head and a more rounded body than the other rorquals. Thus, the humpback is a slower swimmer than its cousins.

Scientists have given the name *Megaptera novaeangliae* to the humpback. This means "big-winged New Englander." The "big wings" refer to the humpback's long flippers. Flippers can grow to sixteen feet (4.8 m) long. The common name "humpback," however, comes from the way the whale dives. A diving humpback leaps out of the water, then it bends its body and enters the water head first. A round "hump" appears as the whale's back disappears.

Most humpbacks belong to one of three separate herds. One herd lives in the North Atlantic. Another can be found in the North Pacific. The third lives below the equator in Antarctic waters. They follow a yearly migration route that takes them from freezing polar waters to warm seas near the equator. This route is thousands of miles long.

Humpbacks make elephants look tiny

A typical male humpback measures forty-eight feet long (14.6 m). It weighs thirty-five to forty-five tons (30,000-40,000 kg). Females are larger. An average female grows to fifty feet long (15.2 m). She weighs about the same as the male. A few females may even grow to sixty feet (18.2 m) or more. Any way you look at it, that's big. The average humpback whale weighs more than six elephants!

As with most whales, humpbacks are black on top and white underneath. Each humpback has white markings on its flukes, or tail fins. Like fingerprints, each set of markings is different. These marks help whale watchers tell one humpback from another. It's almost impossible, however, to tell males from females. Their sex organs are hidden in slits near the tail.

The humpback's skin shows countless round scars left by barnacles. Other scars are left by the bites of small sharks. Humpbacks also have bumps on their upper and lower jaws. One or two stiff hairs grow out of each bump. Biologists think these hairs help the humpback judge its movements through the water.

Humpbacks feed on krill

The huge humpback feeds on some of the sea's smallest creatures. Along with small fish, they catch shrimp-like animals called krill. In turn, the krill

Humpbacks feed on schools of small fish. The fish in this photo are capelin.

feed on the even smaller plankton. It takes ten pounds of plankton to grow a pound of krill — and a humpback needs ten pounds of food to add a pound of weight. Hungry humpbacks can eat three thousand pounds (1,360 kg) of krill and small fish a day!

Humpbacks don't have teeth to chew their food. Instead, their mouth has hundreds of growths on each side called baleen plates. Baleen is a hard material similar to your fingernails. Each plate is covered with a fringe of hair-like fibers. When the humpback opens its mouth, the plates look like a huge, hairy doormat. The baleen plates serve as a food trap.

Humpbacks swim through a school of krill or small fish with their mouths open. They scoop up mouthfuls of water along with the live food. The grooves under the throat expand and make the mouth larger. The fish or krill dart around and get tangled in the fibers on the baleen plates. The whale then shuts its mouth. Its huge tongue squirts the water out and the whale swallows its catch.

Krill often scatter when whales are nearby. When that happens, humpbacks have been seen using bubbles to round up a meal. First, the humpback dives to about fifty feet (15 m). Then the whale swims upward in a wide circle, blowing bubbles from its blowhole. The bubbles make a "net" that slowly drifts upward. The krill are caught in this "net." Then the humpback swims into the crowd of krill to eat its dinner.

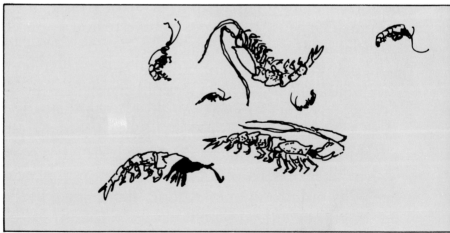

Whales often feed on shrimp-like animals called krill.

Humpbacks are playful creatures

Humpbacks are among the sea's most playful creatures. Families race and jump together. They dive, splash, and slap the water with their flukes. A humpback's tail slap sounds like a rifle shot. Perhaps that sharp noise alerts other whales to danger. The sound made by those great flukes carries a long way.

Humpbacks are often seen jumping out of the water. They roll over in the air and splash down on their backs. Forty tons of whale hitting the water sends spray high in the air. Some whale experts say that these jumps have a purpose. They think the jumps may knock some barnacles loose from the whale's skin.

Humpbacks fill the sea with music

Not long ago, an orchestra played a new piece of music. A tape recorder played along with the musicians. No one had ever heard music like it before. The orchestra's music was written by a human. The tape recorder was playing the "song" of the humpback whale.

Humpbacks have long filled the seas with their "songs." The songs don't carry into the air, however. People didn't hear the music until they began

13

listening under water. Special electronic ears, called hydrophones, pick up the songs. The music is strange and beautiful. People who hear the song of the humpback say they never forget it.

A humpback's song isn't music in the usual sense. The humpback repeats a series of sounds. The song can last from six minutes to half an hour. Sometimes one whale sings alone. At other times, two, three, or more whales join in. The whales do not sing in chorus, however. They all sing the same song, but they start singing at different times.

Some people compare the humpback's song to a bird's song. But birds always sing the same song. Humpbacks change their songs every year! They don't "write" a new song, however. Herds add new parts to the old song. The new parts are sung faster than the old ones. By the third year, the song will have changed even more. Somehow, all the whales in a herd learn the new music.

The songs usually have six parts, called themes. The whales always sing the themes in the same order. Atlantic humpbacks sing different songs than do Pacific herds. But all herds follow the same "rules" for making up their songs.

Humpbacks sing only during the winter months. Singing stops when they reach their cold-water feeding grounds. Perhaps they spend the summer thinking of ways to change their song. When the winter migration starts, new themes appear in last year's

These humpbacks are at their winter feeding grounds in Antarctica.

song. The humpback's songs have even gone into outer space. In 1977, two spaceships lifted off on a trip beyond our solar system. Along with other messages, the Voyagers carried a recording of the humpback's song.

No one knows for sure why or how humpbacks sing. Some experts think the males sing during mating season to attract the females. Perhaps the whales sing just because they like the sounds! Divers report

15

that singing whales don't make bubbles. That means they're not using air to make the sounds. Similarly, we know that humpbacks don't have vocal cords. But they do have a larynx. The larynx is a box at the end of the windpipe. Humpbacks might use air from their lungs to vibrate the larynx to make the sounds. Scientists haven't found a way to look down a live humpback's throat, however. And looking at dead whales hasn't solved the mystery.

In addition to singing, humpbacks grunt, bellow, and whine. Oceanographers are trying to match these sounds with whale behavior. If they can, perhaps they can learn the whale's language. In the meantime, they've learned a lot about the way the humpback's great body works.

Whales "sing" only during the winter months, when they are in warm water.

CHAPTER TWO:

Humpbacks have well developed brains that weigh about eleven pounds (5 kg). That's three times larger than a human brain. Can the humpback solve problems and think like humans? No one knows. Perhaps further study will give us a way to "talk" to these great sea creatures.

A body designed for life in the ocean

Like other large whales, humpbacks take seven years or more to reach adulthood. By their tenth year, they're about eighty-five percent of their full size. No one knows exactly how long they live. A good guess is about fifty years.

For its size, a humpback's skin is quite thin. It is less than one-half inch (1 cm) thick. The smooth surface of the skin helps the whale glide through the water. Sometimes a sick humpback throws itself up on shore. When that happens, the whale gets sunburned! Life in the ocean has left the whale's skin without oil and sweat glands.

Beneath the skin, humpbacks have a thick layer of fat called blubber. This fat is about two feet (.6 m) thick. Blubber gives the whale its rounded shape. The fat also protects the humpback from icy cold water. Without it, whales would freeze in the cold water. Blubber also provides a reserve food supply. These reserves allow the whales to go through the winter months without eating.

The blowhole serves many purposes

Whales live mostly under water, but they breathe air. Their "nose" is a blowhole in the top of their head. The blowhole is divided into two parts like your own nose. During a dive, thick "lips" keep the blowhole closed. After a dive, the blowhole rises out of the water first. A ridge of skin helps hold water away from the blowhole when the "lips" are open.

A humpback "blows" as soon as it surfaces. A spout of air, water, and mucus shoots out of the blowhole. The mucus comes from the whale's lungs. Once the old air is cleared out, the whale takes a number of quick breaths. It looks like a runner panting after a race.

A humpback's spout seldom goes higher than ten feet (3 m). The spout looks like a bushy tree. By contrast, the blue whale's spout rises nearly thirty feet (9 m) high!

A humpback "blows" near the coast of Antarctica.

When they're on the water's surface, humpbacks breathe once every two or three minutes. Before they dive, they take many deep breaths. Humpbacks usually stay under water from three to twenty-five minutes. On deep dives, their bodies withstand water pressures that would crush a human diver. In addition, whales can surface quickly from hundreds of feet down. If human divers came up that fast, nitrogen bubbles would form in their blood. These bubbles can kill a careless diver.

Flippers and flukes serve as paddles

The humpback's flippers are much longer than those of other whales. Long and thin, they extend a third of its length. The front edges are wavy rather than straight. These powerful flippers act as paddles to steer the humpback through the water. Each flipper contains bones that look like a hand. That's because the whale's ancestors had four legs and lived on land thousands of years ago. When these early

The two halves of the humpback's tail are called flukes. The markings on the flukes are different on each humpback.

20

mammals returned to the water, nature slowly changed their front legs and feet into flippers.

Up-and-down movements of the tail speed the humpback on its way. The two halves of the tail are called flukes. Like the flippers, the flukes have uneven, wavy edges. Unlike the flippers, the flukes don't have any bones for support. They are made up of tough muscle tissue. Together, the two flukes measure up to eighteen feet (5.5 m) across. The humpback also has a small dorsal fin on its back. From a distance this fin looks like a shark fin.

Humpbacks swim at a slow two to four miles per hour (3-6 kph). When they have to, however, they can swim much faster. A flip of that powerful tail also sends the humpback leaping high out of the water. They can even do a backflip.

That power is important to the humpbacks. If they weren't such good swimmers, they couldn't make the long migrations which are part of their yearly life cycle.

CHAPTER THREE:

Let's follow the North Pacific herd through its yearly life cycle.

Each summer, two to three thousand humpbacks feed in cold Arctic seas. When winter nears, they migrate south to Hawaii. The visit lasts from December to April. The females give birth to their calves during those months. Spring sends them back to their feeding grounds in the Bering Sea.

Other herds follow a similar schedule. North Atlantic humpbacks can be seen in the West Indies from January to March. Others appear off Bermuda from April to May. Southern hemisphere herds feed in Antarctic waters. During the winter, they migrate northward. Their calving areas are around Australia, Samoa, Ecuador, Brazil, and Africa.

Humpbacks are social creatures

Humpbacks travel in family groups. The young males lead the way. Older males follow, with females and calves bringing up the rear. The various family groups scatter over miles of ocean. They stay in contact with other groups by "singing" to each other. Sound travels well in water. Oceanographers believe that whales can hear the "songs" from many miles away.

Mating takes place in the warm waters of the winter range. Males and females enjoy a playful courtship. A number of whales may begin by racing across the surface of a shallow bay. They splash, jump and slap the water with their tails. The slap of their flippers can be heard for miles. As the courting heats up, the males crash into each other. Their huge flukes lash the water into bubbling foam.

Finally, a male and female humpback pair off. Belly to belly, they rise part way out of the water with their flippers locked together. Mating takes place at this time.

Calves grow quickly

Females carry their unborn calves for eleven to twelve months. Their mating cycle usually produces a calf every other year. A few females give birth every year. This schedule means that calves will always be born in warm waters. Only one calf is born at a time. Twin births are very rare.

No one has ever seen a humpback give birth. Scientists think that calves are born tail first. If they were born head first, they might breathe in some water and drown. A newborn calf averages sixteen feet (5 m) in length. The big calf needs help, or it will

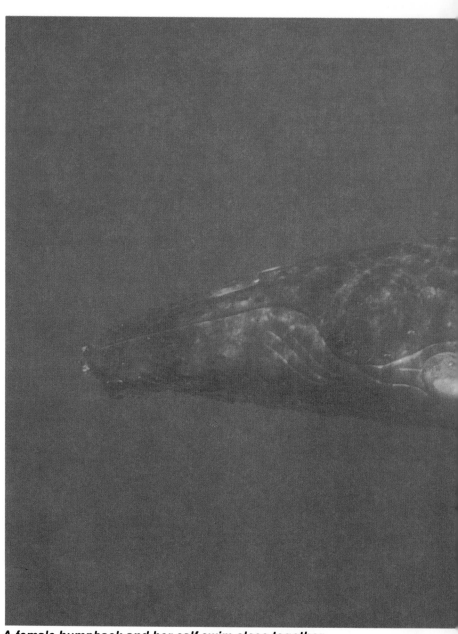

A female humpback and her calf swim close together.

sink. The mother pushes it up to the surface. Sometimes other females come by to help out. The calf soon starts breathing and swimming on its own.

Females nurse their calves like any other mammal. But life in the ocean makes nursing difficult. The mother turns on her side. Her two teats are located in slits near her tail. The calf holds on to one teat, then the mother squirts milk into its mouth. Whale milk contains forty percent fat. By comparison, most cow's milk has about four percent fat. Humpback mothers produce over one thousand pounds (450 kg) of milk a day! You can see why calves can double their weight in a week.

Calves nurse for up to six months. By that time, they're half their adult size. These are busy months. The calf practices diving, leaping, and holding its breath. Instinct helps make these skills easier to learn. As it gets older, the calf also learns how to feed on krill and small fish.

The mothers take good care of their calves. If the calf is in trouble, the mother will stay nearby. Adult humpbacks have been seen pushing a sick calf to the surface so it can breathe.

This protective behavior showed clearly the day a calf was hit by a motorboat off Maui. The calf wasn't hurt badly, but its distress cries brought other whales to the rescue. The people in the motorboat wanted to stay around to watch. They changed their minds when the whales moved between the boat and the calf. One flip of those giant tails could have smashed the small boat.

A busy summer

A calf continues its schooling with a visit to Arctic waters. The calf stops taking milk at about six months of age. The northern waters are full of food. This makes the change of diet fairly easy for the calf. All through the summer, young and old alike stuff themselves with krill and small fish. But the whales will swallow almost anything. Scientists once found

Arctic waters are rich with food.

Whales are sometimes caught in fishing nets. The nets often have to be cut to free the whales.

six fish-eating birds in a humpback's stomach! The whale must have swallowed the birds when it scooped up a school of fish the birds were feeding on.

Summer is also a time when humpbacks get into different kinds of trouble. For example, whales may run into large nets put out to catch cod. Once they get tangled in the nets, they do many dollars worth of damage. The cod fishers sometimes have to cut the nets to free the whales. Late in the summer, a few humpbacks may get caught in the shifting Arctic ice. If the ice doesn't break up in time, the whales will starve.

A migrating herd

A humpback herd may number as many as a hundred whales. The herd spreads out as it travels. If it didn't there wouldn't be enough food. When one group of whales finds a rich supply of krill, they slap the water with their flippers. The loud noise soon brings other humpbacks to share in the feast.

Sea birds and porpoises follow the herd. The sea birds know that smaller fish scatter as the humpbacks pass by. When the fish come to the surface, the birds dive and catch them. By contrast, the speedy porpoises seem to be there to have fun. They often ride waves created by the slow-moving humpbacks.

If whales studied people, they'd wonder about our

strange habits. Why do we sleep everyday? Humpbacks don't sleep during their five-thousand-mile migrations. They catch up on their sleep at the end of the trip. A sleeping whale floats near the surface. The head and flukes hang down limply. They rise up every ten minutes to take a breath. A number of boats have been wrecked by running into sleeping whales.

Even whales have predators

The ocean is full of predators, but only killer whales and sharks attack the humpback. A team of fierce killer whales once caught up with a herd as it neared Arctic waters. Two killer whales bit into the flippers of an old male who was swimming alone. While the humpback was held helpless, a third killer whale bit savagely at the larger whale's mouth. The killer whale was after the humpback's tongue. If the killer whales had been successful, the humpback would have died. This time, the tough old humpback plunged and twisted. The whale finally shook off his attackers. Scarred and bloody, he was able to swim back to the herd.

Large sharks follow the herd, waiting to pick off a sick or crippled humpback. One small shark, however, goes after humpbacks like a mosquito goes after people. Known as the cookie-cutter shark, it sneaks in from behind and bites round chunks out of the whale's skin. The bites are a nuisance, but they never kill the whale.

Several types of small hitchhikers also annoy the giant humpbacks. Whale lice crawl around on the whale's skin. Lampreys and remoras often stick tightly to the whales. They are a bigger problem. These eel-like creatures live by sucking the whale's blood. Barnacles can also be a serious problem. At

This humpback has barnacles growing on its skin.

least three types of barnacles grow on the whale's tail, throat, and flippers. The barnacles feed on plankton, so they don't bleed the whale. But adult humpbacks can be weighed down with up to one thousand pounds (453 kg) of barnacles!

A strange rescue

An unusual incident marked one herd's migration back to Arctic waters. Parasites had infected a young female's inner ear. The infection upset her sense of direction. Unable to dive and surface properly, she swam into shallow water near a busy swimming beach. When the tide went out, she was stranded. While people watched in amazement, six other humpbacks beached themselves near the dying female. It seemed as though they were trying to comfort her. But without the water to help support their huge bulk, the whales couldn't breathe properly.

The news spread quickly. A naturalist rounded up some powerful motorboats. The crews tied ropes to the whales and dragged them back out to sea. The female died, but the other humpbacks were saved by the rescue effort.

The sight of people saving whales marks a new chapter in the story of this beautiful animal. In the past, people only killed whales.

CHAPTER FOUR:

Some people say that whales don't know very much. All they do is swim around, having fun. They live at peace with their habitat.

Maybe that's the point. Many humans don't seem to be at peace with themselves. Perhaps we can learn something from the humpbacks. But first, we have to make sure they survive.

Humpbacks were easy game

Humans have hunted the humpback for over a thousand years. The Indians of North America were among the earliest whalers. Coastal Indians chased the humpbacks and other whales in bark canoes. They killed the huge animals with barbed spears called harpoons. The Indians used every part of their catch. They ate the meat and burned the oil for light and heat. Whalebone made a good framework for building huts and sleds. Baleen was carved into jewelry.

The Basques of Spain were Europe's first whalers. They hunted humpbacks in the Bay of Biscay. In the 1500's, the Basques often followed the herds north to Greenland. The Basque whalers only wanted the blubber, which gave them a clean-burning fuel. They threw the rest of the whale into the sea.

Modern whaling began in New England

Some of the Europeans who settled America also turned to whaling. Large whaling ports appeared in Massachusetts, on Nantucket Island and at New Bedford. Unlike the Indians, these whalers didn't wait for the annual migration of the herds. They sailed as far as the South Atlantic hunting the whale. Profits were high. People all over the world wanted whale oil.

Whaling as it appeared in early times.

Each of the early whaling ships carried four or five smaller boats. These boats were about thirty feet (9 m) long. Each boat carried a crew of six. Four whalers rowed, one steered, and the harpooner stood at the bow. It was his job to throw the harpoon. After he hit a whale, the harpooner poured buckets of water on the rope tied to the harpoon. That was important, because a harpooned whale pulled out many yards of rope. The heat built up by a dry rope rubbing on the boat sometimes started a fire.

When a whaling ship's lookout saw humpbacks, the sailors set off in their small boats. They rowed quietly into the herd. When a whale came up to breathe, the harpooner threw the harpoon. The barbs held the point deep in the whale's body. A harpooned humpback usually took off at high speed, towing the boat with it. Whalers called this wild trip a "Nantucket sleigh ride."

Finally, the humpback tired and came to the surface. This gave the rowers a chance to get close. The harpooner then stuck a pointed lance into the whale's lungs. This often sent the dying whale into a final frenzy. Quickly, the rowers backed the boat away. One blow from the giant flukes could crush the boat.

Humpbacks sink after they die. To prevent this, the whalers tied air-filled bags to the body of the dying whale. Then they towed the whale to the whaling ship. There, the crew jumped down to the floating body. They stripped off the blubber with long, sharp knives. On deck, other men cut the blubber into smaller pieces. A fire was built under large pots to "try" out the oil. The pure oil was then stored in barrels. The rest of the body was left for the sharks.

Humpbacks slide toward extinction

Whalers from other countries also hunted the giant mammals. But whales were not easy to find. A whaling trip sometimes lasted for two years or more. Any whale would do, but whalers found that humpbacks were easy to kill. These slow-moving giants never learned to stay away from humans with harpoons.

The killing went on and on. In winter, whalers followed the herds southward into warmer waters. When summer came, the killing began again in cold water feeding areas. Between 1904 and 1939, whalers killed over 100,000 humpbacks in southern waters. Thousands more were killed in the north. In the Pacific, Maui, in the Hawaiian Islands, became a major whaling port. In the southern hemisphere, Australia was an important whaling center.

Humpbacks are easy targets

Of all the whales taken by the whalers, the humpback was the unluckiest. For one thing, their oil doesn't burn as well as that of other whales. Old-time whalers made up for that by killing more of them. To make it worse, all of the humpback's habits made it easy to catch. Whalers could wait for the herd to return to its feeding grounds. Or, they could hunt the whales at their warm-water mating areas. To make it even easier, the slow-swimming humpbacks were often found near shore.

A research ship moves along right next to a slow-moving humpback.

If the killing had kept on, the humpback would be extinct today. But people saw the danger just in time. They began saying, "Save the whales!"

Nations join to limit whaling

In 1946, a number of countries formed the International Whaling Commission (IWC). The IWC tried to save the whales by making rules. One rule limited the months when whales could be killed. Whalers were also told to stay out of waters where calves were being born. They were asked not to kill small whales.

In 1946, the International Whaling Commission asked whalers to stay out of certain areas when calving occurs.

The IWC made good rules. But some of the whaling nations refused to obey them. In 1961, the IWC tried to stop the killing of humpbacks in parts of the Antarctic. But Japan, Russia, and Norway refused to stop. If a whaling ship killed a protected whale, the IWC fined its captain. The fines were too small to do much good.

Despite these defeats, some victories have been won. In 1966, the IWC gave humpbacks special protection and most whalers stopped hunting them. Further, the United States scrapped its whaling fleet in 1971. Countries that still kill whales cannot sell whale products in this country. Great Britain, Iceland, and Holland have also stopped killing whales.

In 1973, the United Nations asked all nations to stop killing whales. The IWC also voted for a total end to whaling by 1988. But the killing still goes on. The UN and the IWC can't enforce their rules.

The failure of the IWC and the UN has led the non-whaling nations to take action of their own. The U.S., for example, has told Russia and Japan to get rid of their whaling fleets. If they don't, U.S. fishing grounds will be closed to them. In addition, non-whaling countries might refuse to buy goods from the whaling countries. If no one buys their products, Japan and Russia might obey the IWC's rules. But boycotts are hard to enforce. Very few Americans want to stop buying Japanese cars and other products.

Whaling is finally dying out

If laws won't save whales, perhaps money will. A whale is worth about $10,000, but whales are hard to find these days. Hunting the few that are left doesn't return big profits any more. Even so, Japan says that her people need whale meat.

Only a few countries, including Russia, Norway, and Japan, still allow whaling. The Japanese whaling fleets are like floating factories. The fleet has special ships for each job. Airplanes fly above the herds and radio back their locations. Fast ships then chase the whales. Gunners use cannons to fire exploding harpoons. A harpoon, that kills the whale with electric shock, has also been used.

The killer ships tow the bodies to the parent ship. These ships are big enough to take an entire whale aboard. The crew cuts up the body. Blubber is turned into oil, and the meat is frozen to keep it fresh. IWC observers on the factory ships try to make sure that the whalers don't kill humpbacks and other protected whales.

It appears that no one really needs whale oil, meat, and bone today. Whale oil can be replaced by petroleum or vegetable oils. As for whale meat, few people outside Japan and Russia eat it. Whales killed today often end up as food for dogs and minks. And whale

A diver swims near whale bones. In the past, whale bone was used to make fertilizer.

bone doesn't need to be made into fertilizer. Cheaper fertilizers can be made easily from other materials.

Why does the hunting go on? There are several reasons. Whaling means jobs for whalers, and whale products for people who like them. The whaling countries have a lot of money invested in ships and equipment. It's also hard to give up old customs.

Private groups join the battle

Private citizens have joined the fight to save the whales. Some of these conservation groups include

A curious humpback swims near some small boats.

Greenpeace, Friends of the Earth, Project Jonah, and the American Cetacean Society. These groups make people aware of the problem. They raise money and write letters to lawmakers. This puts pressure on their governments.

Greenpeace goes a step further. Its members believe in action. The group sends out boats to make sure that whalers don't kill protected whales. The Greenpeace sailors steer their small boats between the whales and the whaler's harpoons. One Green-

A humpback jumps out of the water off the coast of Newfoundland.

peace group even landed in Siberia. While there, they handed out anti-whaling leaflets to workers at a whale products plant. The Russians weren't amused. They put the Greenpeace people in jail for a week.

These stunts make headlines. Greenpeace hopes this will help save the whales.

Do humpbacks have a future?

People who love the whales are working to get even tougher laws passed to protect them. Conservationists want to save the beautiful singing whales for the future.

Experts say we must give the humpback a hundred years. That's how long it will take the herds to grow back to full size. Given that time, they believe the gentle giant can win its battle for survival.

The fight isn't over. Let's hope we can soon say to the humpbacks: "That was a close one. We almost lost you. Finally, we've thrown away the last harpoon."

MAP:

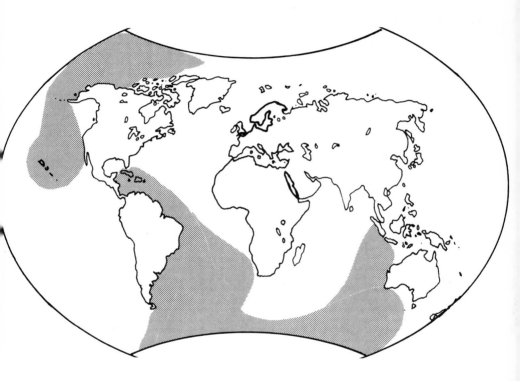

The shaded areas
show where most
humpbacks live.

INDEX/GLOSSARY:

INDEX/GLOSSARY:

WILDLIFE
HABITS & HABITAT

READ AND ENJOY THE SERIES:

If you would like to know more about all kinds of wildlife, you should take a look at the other books in this series.

You'll find books on bald eagles and other birds. Books on alligators and other reptiles. There are books about deer and other big-game animals. And there are books about sharks and other creatures that live in the ocean.

In all of the books you will learn that life in the wild is not easy. But you will also learn what people can do to help wildlife survive. So read on!